Y0-BKG-424

# Discovering Mortality

## Bruce Lader

Copyright © 2005
Bruce Lader
March Street Press
3413 Wilshire Dr.
Greensboro NC 27408-2923
336 282 9754
rbixby@earthlink.net
http://www.marchstreetpress.com
isbn 1-59661-026-3

author photo by Renata Lader

# Contents

## I

Trespasser 3
Rules 4
Recital 5
A Minute to Twilight 7
Betrayed 9
Spies 11
Sabotage 13
Ceremony 14
Secrets 15
Emperor of Baseball 17
Wait Till You're Twenty-One 19
In the World Series of Jazz 20
Twelfth Summer 22
Lava Beds, Hawaii 23

## II

Vibes 27
Liar 29
In Between 30
Splitting Wood 31
Where It Is 33
Property 34
Detour 35
Murder in the Dunes 37
Thieves 38
Death Hand 40

## III

Playground Keeper   43
Puzzle   45
Fame   47
The Boy Who Loved to Fish   48
From a Boy's Home   49
Discovering Mortality   50
The Hustle   51
Advice from a Bag Lady   53
Excuses   54
Lunch Hour   55
Siege   56
Empty   58


## IV

Testamentary   61
Renascent Elegy   63
Plans   66
Nest-Egg   68
Doing Time   69
Fragments of War   71
Casualties   72
That Mysterious Yearned-For Person   73
Sunflower Fever   75
Vows   76
On a Plane from Yellowstone   78
The Claim   80

# Acknowledgments

Grateful acknowledgment is made to the editors of the journals in which the following poems, several in slightly different form, first appeared:

*Aim*: "Casualties"
*The Antigonish Review*: "Splitting Wood"
*Confrontation*: "Trespasser"
*Controlled Burn*: "Death Hand"
*Earth First*: "On a Plane from Yellowstone"
*Fulcrum*: "Empty" and "From a Boy's Home"
*Green Hills Literary Lantern*: "Lunch Hour"
*The Hawaii Review*: "Ceremony" and "Excuses"
*Iodine Poetry Journal*: "Fragments of War"
*International Poetry Review*: "Doing Time"
*The Listening Eye*: "In the World Series of Jazz"
*Main Street Rag*: "The Hustle"
*The Malahat Review*: "Recital"
*Manzanita Quarterly*: "The Claim"
*MARGIE*: "Fame"
*New Millennium Writings*: "Sunflower Fever"
*The New York Quarterly*: "Murder in the Dunes"
*Poet Lore*: "Puzzle"
*Poetry*: "Wait Till You're Twenty-One"
*Poetry Salzburg Review*: "The Boy Who Loved to Fish"
*The Potomac Review*: "Siege"
*The Powhatan Review*: "Advice from a Bag Lady"
*RE:AL*: "Detour"
*The Roanoke Review*: "Emperor of Baseball"
*The Rockford Review*: "Sabotage"
*Sojourn*: "Thieves"

*Talking River Review*: "Lava Beds, Hawaii"
*Tulane Review*: "Plans"
*The Vanderbilt Review*: "Rules"

"Secrets" appeared in the *Poetic Voices Without Borders* anthology (Gival Press, 2005).

My thanks to the Helene Wurlitzer Colony where some of these poems were written, and to the College of Creative Studies at the University of California-Santa Barbara for an honorarium. Many thanks also to my caring readers in The Washington Street Writers' Group.

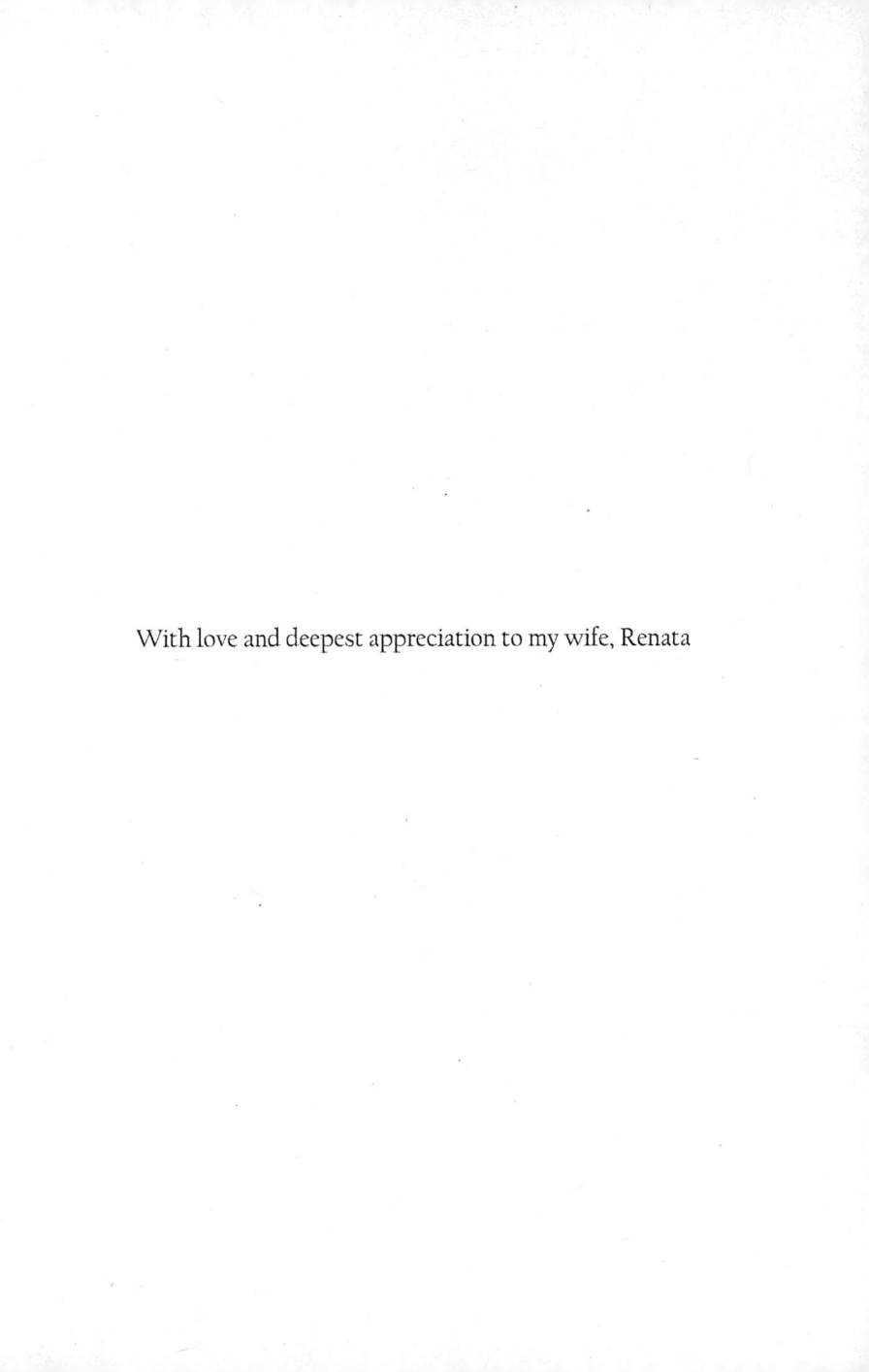

With love and deepest appreciation to my wife, Renata

I

## Trespasser

He comes in my room without knocking,
opens the shade. My father would have
killed me for that. He should know better
than wake me up and risk my anger. *Dad look
how deep the snow is.* It hasn't entered
his lazy mind that I was in my office
again till four o'clock working accounts,
then couldn't fall asleep. Maybe if
I get out of bed, look out the window,
he'll be satisfied and go away,
let me snooze the rest of this Valium.
Then I will have the strength to work, and give him
things my father only dreamed of.
Those are footprints where he's
been prowling. The mess is piled like pages
over everything. *Dad, I'm tracking down
a dangerous animal.* What can I do
differently than my father who was always
too tired from tailoring to welcome me?
On the back of a business card,
I write Detective, my boy's name, a by-line
that sounds official. He throws his arms around me,
runs off into silence, a shadow stalking
a shadow who terrifies him, like the stranger
in the prosperity of his own house.

# Rules

*Don't you come in the house
with berries on your shoes*
my mother warned when,
sticky juice on my fingers,
oozing down my arms
from nibbling mulberry tendrils,
weaving them like a Maypole,

I trekked in berry juice,
begging to keep another
stray dog or cat. Suddenly
she tore after me
screaming *I'm gonna kill you.*

I didn't know she could
run so fast. Terrified
I dodged out the door
a squirrel to the maple tree,
by the hair of a wobbly tooth
got the '56 Fairlane between us
like "the monkey chased the weasel,"

saved an ear from being bitten off,
then hunkered in my tepee
under the blue spruce,
praying she wouldn't blab.

But when dinnertime dragged me
inside like a dog who knew better,
she laughed at my purple-smudged face,
called me *wild Indian*,
had cleaned up every trace.

## Recital

Here is going to play music soon.
My hair is washed and nice is why
and my clothes are new.

I sit in the front row
right in the middle by myself.
I'm allowed tonight like nobody brought me.

Look up. A star comes in like the movies.
Everybody clap. Fancy red dress lady pretty.

No talk.
Can't wait to start.
*Sh* to see music.

Now she says with the horn.
Also her hair is shiny brown.
Silk makes a sound.
Two long skinny braids like an angel.

They said what she plays.
Oboe.
Shouldn't laugh because no giggles I promised have.

Scared I will. Scrunch down low in seat
they can't see get mad.
She tries hard. Face red puffs. I bite my tongue.
Frog cheeks. No help to hold serious in.
I bust.

Been bad. Can't stay up late next time.
They don't love me again anymore. Much sad.
Worst is they know I can never reach grownup.

# A Minute to Twilight

In sunbeams alongside the hedges,
horizon-stretch, stand
a frozen statue,
soon you're a magnet
red admirals land on.

Whistling a vibrating leaf
that tickles the mouth to let go,
skip in the abandoned lots
where a ton of quartz rock
is a dinosaur egg.

With a swift fist
uppercut the ball higher
than the rainbow branch
of the giant sycamore bridging
hide-and-seek field.

Hop the bike named Express
and follow it with a sesame wish
past polliwog woods.

Divide a sappy propeller pod
off the maple.
Spin dizzy a thousand

times a thousand fireflies
then glue it on the nose like a fin.

At the top of Danger Mountain
take a toboggan glide
like a ball rollercoasters
a garden hose track.
Steer an ice cream stick ship
down thunderstorm river.

# Betrayed

The world he played in was a new puppy someone grabbed
ripped out of him he couldn't stop screaming a silent gasp
of a million alarms of terror his arms froze in a cradle
legs in quicksand nightmare couldn't run to rescue

Mother stood in the driveway by the side door watching
he looked at her in disbelief pleaded *hurry stop the kidnappers
stole part of my body in that car hurry bring it back or I will die
kill me instead of my only friend* and she whispered *sorry*

he did a terribly wrong thing so suddenly the strength
to keep her grownup power to love and protect was lost
but it was just as wrong to tell him lies break the promise
that he could keep the stray if he'd care for him walk Boots

enough to live up to his end of the deal but how could
a seven-year-old with no brother or sister do everything
without help find a field where a beagle could have space
to run and point when he wasn't allowed to leave the block

He yelled to his father in the basement there was no voice
he had abandoned his office when needed the most
his son was being crushed and the coward wasn't home
had conspired with the enemy as a flood of anger seized him

they had gone through with their threats secretly arranged
to give him to a family that could love and care for him
smaller than an ant crazy with grief he crawled to
an unfamiliar house of betrayal slithered down a dark

hole buried the brutal bone in a closet in a room of distrust
locked every door and window marked with their two hearts
the last sound he made a desperate howl as he looked
for him in futile places he had disappeared forever.

## Spies

Quadruple dared by the alpha bully
on our block, bored in dog days to the brink
of senseless mischief, we snaked in shady
clothes of night, cat-climbed rickety fences,
boosted one another up the retaining wall
in back of my garage, covered in branches
of apple tree where we'd escape to trade
baseball cards, try to understand positions
and techniques in the marriage manual
stolen for capers of prepubescent laughter
from indiscreet parents. *Don't stare, it's rude*,
they'd scold when we'd observe the delicate
woman in the wheelchair, curious to know
why legs were burdened with heavy braces.

Taking turns, we trudged up the garage roof
steeper than sledding Suicide Hill,
frightened one sound could alarm neighbors
in the manicured suburb, stood at the level
of her second story apartment window
wide open for a breeze of relief from heat.
Binocular burglars in a forbidden
private world, we focused on her silver-framed
glow from the TV, out of the wheelchair,
snug in her husband's lap on the couch,
naked arms clinging to his neck, wearing
a see-through nightgown. High on bravado,
tittering as they fondled, we jostled and
fumbled the binoculars onto the tiles.

A flood of light from their window blinded us
down the roof into the moonless dark
like roaches scattering for secret crevices
of crime nests. *Get off my property, go away,*
I yelled, forsaking my accomplices, panic
undermining conviction, a cruel coward
cornered in an evil act with his ridiculous alibi,
scrambling to salvage a semblance of dignity
and divert adult fingers of blame. Our hideaway
of innocence exposed, trapped in a jail
of pornographic guilt, we dreaded a word
from the couple meaning the third degree,
no home would harbor boys manacled
in shame, nothing would be normal again.

## Sabotage

As I proudly conducted the Seder, began
to recite the prayers, he watched with a smile
I couldn't decipher, yarmulke doming waves
of jet hair, to my dismay drank wine, took
a bite of matzah, dipped parsley in salt water,
out of correct order. "No, Dad, not yet"
I pleaded, humiliated to a mute speck of vengeance
masking tears from that hero who had fought robbers,
fisted the gunman, landed a solid blow
around an eye before they slugged him down,
wrestled work hours away, screeched rubber
through a hole in the night. He was teaching me
to value a drop of his sweat, so I would
understand even bitter roots can yield
a garden, the hard-earned righteousness of study.

# Ceremony

Witchhazel redolent, my grandfather
would perform his orange mouthpiece
and bubbling oatmeal breakfast,
pull magnifying glass from vest,
finger-lick the Yiddish *Forward:*
Soviets Bang a Teakettle,
Elderly Vetoed by Filibuster.

"More nourishing bread in this world
than education, boychik, there isn't"
he'd say, laughing about another juicy
episode of Bashevis Singer, folding pages
carefully, the way he'd steam-press
thousands of garments in the sweatshop
and make handkerchief squirrels

leap from his hands. Astounding me
with cigar smoke-ring stories of his circus
adolescence in Bessarabia—entire villages
burned to the ground in Cossack
pogroms that killed brothers and sisters—
Harry would trace lost childhood
tunes on piano, take me to matinees
at the RKO, turn an empty Chiclet's pack
into a shofar. On a constitutional
to bring *The Post, The Mirror,
The Herald Tribune,* a loaf *challa,*
he'd bless doctors, freedom, and the Yanks,
curse anti-unionists, right-wing senators,
any no-goodnik who'd get on his nerves.

# Secrets

Dora had no need for the meshugga language
I was learning, relatives and friends
were landsmen who understood. When I'd ask
about her youth, she'd say, hands trembling
with Parkinson's, "*Zeis kind*, I didn't
go to *shul*; you learn Yiddish."

How in my world of preparing for Bar Mitzvah,
mastering Chopin, and playing baseball,
was I going to preserve a dialect
dwindling like memories of the old country
she preferred to forget? Besides,
the stuff she and my mother gossiped
they wanted to keep secret from me.

Frustrated hearing only the mother tongue
when my grandma was present,
I questioned my grandfather and parents,
trying to gather elusive fragments—
like belongings abandoned in Romania—
of the world everyone else wanted to leave,
and they took me to task for being a *nudzh*.

I listened between the notes of joyous
folk singing for clues of the woman
who had shared her small Hester Street
apartment with a homeless immigrant,
brought the child up a second daughter;
I studied photos of her in London at fifteen,
sunning with cousins, footloose with laughing
girlfriends in the Catskills; I watched her

work the sewing machine, arthritic fingers
agile as they crafted miles of thread,
embroidered blouses, aprons, kerchiefs
she would give to friends. I remember
her stoical *tsuris*, love translated
into cooking beyond belief, the freedom
in Zion America she'd say means everything.

Notes:

Zeis kind: sweet child
Shul: school
Nudzh: pest
Tsuris: troubles

## Emperor of Baseball

My lightning wrist-snap swing
dented the cowhide
distances kids twice my size
wished they could equal.
Heretic of schoolyards
who played hooky from synagogue,
my controlled repertoire
of wicked curves
bewildered leagues of hoods.

Resilient as an acrobat on a trampoline,
pockets bulging fire engine berries,
I squirreled the autumn dogwood,
malingered piano practice
for tryouts with the Yankees,
homered seven roofs
beyond the neighbor's apple tree
with a broomstick.

My delinquency targeted
a statue's dangling lantern,
bullseyed thunderous pieces
of my father's mind
with a laser snowball,
a line-drive walloped
through our stained-glass window.

Chewing wads of Bazooka,
I gloved a dream of glory
as fireflies kindled evening,
circled the diamonds
in my empire of baseball
like a backwards clock.

# Wait Till You're Twenty-One

All day down in the salt mine basement
his clients visit, lodge brothers
he embraces with the gift of gab,
as if it's been ages since the nights
they kibitzed pinochle, gin rummy,
and bridge. He loves them more than me,
his number-one trophy. At last,
they've gone, but he's busy together
with unending work and classical music
as friends. He needs the debit
of this no-account, disrespectful teen
like mortgage payments. He swishes
a glass of Lipton, smokes another Camel,
plots the maps of their fiscal lives,
saving them taxes. He brags the balance
is a happy medium like Mendelssohn's
*Italian Symphony* playing. It vexes him
that I sulk so much, when he's providing
the time to myself he didn't have.

# In the World Series of Jazz

The pitcher walks straight ahead to the mound,
taps his foot in front of the stand,
licks the reed a taste or two
looks in for a sign and
before breathing a sound
lets the rhythm grab him,
gets into a groove.

The monster in the lineup
points the club, ready to swing the charts
like Bechet, Prez, and Benny,
or hard bop the ball out of the park
like Bird, sensing vibes the hurler phrases
from his medley of instant surprises

but the dot blows by, a goose egg of smoke
burning the catcher's mitt,
and then a Kansas City slider
side-slips the plate, explodes runs of blues.

The joint of eighty thousand plus
jumps like grasshoppers in a field of butterflies,
logic laid out,
as the cat tempts a half-speed change,
a curve bridged above his wheelhouse
like a slow boat to China, but the batter,
cool as Monk, Gerry, and Chet,
doesn't chase the quote.

The players are off their benches
as the southpaw winds, spins loose
a dexterous swallow of joy, the agile
turnaround of a tune
to take us out.

# Twelfth Summer

*...nothing will ever dazzle you
like the dreams of your body...*
—Mary Oliver

To let him slide his hand nervously
up an arm, nestle it in the soft
valley next to her breast, his cheek
touching shoulder smooth
as dolphin skin while he pretended
to doze, intoxicated by woman's
deodorant as they traveled on,
she had to love him, he thought,
wishing they would never stop,
planning to give the sixteen-year-old
cuddled against him, eyes closed,
a flower to float in her watery hair
if the animal pulling them in the white
river of its hunger ever slowed down, if
it ever released them from the dream
they desired to grasp like fragrant
fruits of a tree they were clinging to when
a shadow of wingspan scythed through
the field of grass dancing with wind
and the eagle blended in dark folds
of wood the way she looked in his
naive eyes, stared as long as he didn't
turn, having to know he wanted her
to awaken him with her gift of knowledge.

## Lava Beds, Hawaii

A river of white grass
          sways in the wind
      down a turn in ravine
of black volcanic ground,

the small flames of grass
      a crowd of bright candles
           lifted through a cloud of light
      cradled between cliffs
where lava flowed.

Shadows of cliffs resemble
      dark clouds reflected in water
           under gray border of sky.

      Everything growing
on this primordial terrain
      is grass erupted in glowing
           hillocks of higher and higher flames

      as I look over a slant ridge
and the river of fire flows
      toward me, scrawling
           a signature of genesis on earth.

II

## Vibes

I notice he forgot to fasten
a button on my favorite shirt,
the wounded puppy look,
uncombed cowlick.

The extravagant bouquet
with another new sex toy gift
is supposed to make up
for everything again.

He says it's silly, manipulative
and hurts him when I get so upset,
wipes away my tears
with promises we're one.

I open the package, unfold
the red camisole from Victoria's Secret
and soon the insensitive
things that naughty boy has done

have slipped my mind
my mind is gone. How long
does he think he can
keep on being so outrageous?

He doesn't have to phone day
and night like my friend he's
jealous of, get down on his knees
and propose, but if he'd only

say he's sorry it would be like
the time he thought of the Tiffany

necklace with my birthstone,
like the Casanova cares,

I'd look in his forgiving eyes
and ask if he wants to move in,
I'd give him all the kinky
love he would ever need.

# Liar

Finally she unwraps the present
she had smacked out of my hand
with a barrage of false indictments

about unfamiliar perfume,
dabbling in the office, flimsy
suspicions no one could defend,

climbs into the lingerie, calmly
repeats her moving-in-together
ultimatum with those voluptuous
eyes that would warm Antarctica,

asks if I love her. Well, I thought
of her jealous friend, the catch-22
she is in for promotion, my sweating
a second job to help raise the kid,
meet payments on the Lexus.

I forgot how she had exploded
*you irresponsible son-of-a-bitch* at me
for being late, didn't know what to say
that was true and wouldn't hurt her.

I saw a tear wander down a cheek
and all I could do was take her
in my arms, and propose.

## In Between

A friend, longing to be more,
I listen to her talk about her lover,
unwilling to believe the sensitive woman
has fallen for a two-timer.

She complains he stood her up,
yet how thoughtful he can be with gifts.
I'm in tears when she says
he's had the arrogance
to flick away her delicate hand.

I have dreamed for years
of holding her close, as if a slim
chance could exist, and she goes on
about their trip to Hawaii, the marvelous
way he dances, how in bed he is a miracle.
The thought of him being with her,
touching her child, annihilates me.

I know I don't have the charm
he has mesmerized her into believing
paves the road to money,
don't have his drive for expensive
things to make her happy,
won't be the man she will always
give her tenderness and love.

# Splitting Wood

I only wanted
to replenish the hearth,
go out to the shed,
select a wood-chunk,
chop,
come back with arms full
to stoke the fire.

The fog lifted,
leaving gray overcast.
Where the block met dank sod,
green mold clung;
a rusted gas can
leaned
on a flat tire.

Between the stiff ribs
I set a steel wedge,
dog-eared
and frayed from having been
forged down
and down
by the weight of the sledge

hammer.
Each heavy, redundant stroke
raised the din
of a blacksmith pounding
his anvil's tongue,
split the pulpy wood
with a torpid

creak.
A coffin opened.
Was the hour rung?
Far off, I heard
a dead man's stifled shriek,
thump of a large tree felled,
a waterfall,

rushing. Softly,
a breeze touched my cheek.
Then something dammed the cataract,
and all was hushed.
The breeze, too, faded away.
The spell that held a spirit's breath,
was broken.

# Where It Is

"I was an R.N. in Victoria General
where they are televising,"
she says on the sofa, watching *General Hospital*.
The coincidence amuses me
as I cover her with a blanket, give her tea,
another pillow, pyramid the fire,

walk snow-shrouded forest
down to Prospect Lake. Her husband drowned
swimming off the island—
that ghost ship with tree-skeleton masts
moored in the center. Was the voice
reaching through my pillow like an alien dream
a message from him?

Mist rises from dark water
like waving arms. I step onto the pier,
encounter myself under the surface
while geese descend in flurries of laughter.
Her turned over canoe and rowboat
are white tortoises hibernating in reeds.

Lucky to have found a secluded
home for my cargo of books and records,
I gather wood to stay afloat,
share meals, listen politely
as her streams of laughing chatter
pull me from harbor in this room.

## Property

Leave that tree alone,
it watches over our lives,
don't saw it down.

You built a sundeck,
can't wait to work on a tan,
so you earmarked the tree
a trespasser in your backyard
obstructing lake view.

Don't spoil that shade,
home of eagles and warblers.
From windows of loss
a friend of redolent fir
will be a missing 17-pointer.

Neighbor standing for
a snapshot on a trophy
of plundered elephantine
hulk, sawdust spurts as you
slice generations of limbs
in a minute, tornado apart
centuries of girth.

You catch a breather
by a mountain of firewood,
savor a smoke.

# Detour
*for Robert Werling*

It wasn't a rock after all,
lying still and black in a valley
between the giant sand-dunes
resembling horizontal human forms.

Recent rains had firmed the surface,
and so the three of us strolled
lightly out on the sleeping flesh

like Lilliputians carrying your tripod,
sack of filmslides filters and meters,
and the bellows camera you accordioned
to deepen the dimensions of dunes.

You weren't interested in that
distant unknown object; you were busy
highlighting the motionless ripples
prevailing onshore winds had fluted
like water of the wetland lakes,

defining with yellow and red filters
the lengthening parabolas of shadow
cast by wavy domes of transverse ridges,

capturing, the way Ansel Adams
and the Westons did, new music
in the abstract simplicity of sand.

We could breathe the sea and hear
its constant susurrus miles beyond
the arches of dunes. Then detouring down

we saw the skull and ravaged neck
of a fetid carcass, splatters of blood
tinting the scuffled sand. It may have
gotten loose from a riding stable.

Perhaps it sensed wilderness
in its unsaddled bones before
coyotes emerged from the scrub,
focused on their prey, and the winds
began the slow process of burial.

# Murder in the Dunes

They didn't dream the dead horse
omened dissolution of their marriage.
They looked for footprints
of coyotes who had hounded
the marrow out of those rifted remains
unfaithful as dunes of strewn
emotions that shift with weather
and tides, but rippling sand
concealed evidence of attackers
like burrowed voles, hares
hiding in brambles, wind over
lake surfaces where tern, loon
and kingfisher dive.

A handful of minutes
would have buried the splotches
of blood in Oceano sand,
finished submerging the unbridled
carcass gnarled as driftwood
sifted down windblown furrows,
but they, infatuated with dunes
higher than tsunamis under spindrift
wings of cirrus, were drawn to the hawk
revolving maelstrom sky.
He pointed to the killer whale,
she, a woman dressed in shadows;
neither wanted to think of their
love in ruins, the war that lurked
like an owl keen to swoop
their dens of separate silence,
leave them stranded in estranged night.

## Thieves

In the pit of a dispute,
fragments of anger
adding up to an echoing
zero, I climb over packed cartons
that wait for our next move,
walk onto the apartment terrace
for a breath,

and notice, below the fuchsia hanging
like a spider from the rafter,
an egg, null as the tomorrow
of living together,
webbed in silent tongues
of ferns. I go back in,

watch through the glass wall
that divides terrace from room,
grasp at straws and slender
twigs of clues spare as the nest,
and the next day find a second egg,
blank as no solution.

The male dove incubates them
beside the flowerboxes tethered
like lifeboats to the railing;
the female sits in the tangled
ivy leaves, then her wings whistle
toward fields of seeds.

At night we guard a violent darkness,
pretend decoys of sleep

outside the expanding territory
of quarrel. The shells soon
separate, wet feathers appear,
but when the parents, lifelong mates,
eyes dark as fertility,
drop the pieces away from the nest,

plundering blue-jays
try to murder the hatchlings,
give us only the vigilance
of cutthroats in common,
moments of suspicious ceasefires
amid knife-pecking accusations.

Now the hungry nestlings
tug at nurturing beaks,
milk the harvest of swallowed
seeds from bloated crops,
while in the famine after sieges
of imprisoning sentences,
we starve for a touch
of iridescent affection.

On their own without feedings,
the fledglings fall
free of the terrace,
new wings beat air into sunlight,
as we look down the road,
thieves going to a different place.

# Death Hand

We were gliding a sleigh.
        I couldn't determine where—
it didn't matter, the weather was heaven
that day, nineteen years after he died,
my father looked the twenties I had only seen
in a rare photo of him.

We held no reins, no advantage
earned or by default.
        His hand, having betrayed work,
cigarettes, bowling, cards, glasses of tea,
was a dream of concordance
realized in mine.

The horses trotted in tandem
effortlessly powerful, as we chatted
freely with total understanding.
        Gone were his fracturing shouts,
my failed wars of vengeful silence.

        His head of gleaming widow's-peaked hair
rested against my fatherly shoulder
a lawless moment. Then, rebellious
man of desire, I woke up.

# III

# Playground Keeper

As the local train of neighbors
drifted in the derelict depot,
I passed a basketball to Stuff.
The ex-talented athlete dribbled
down the tarmac court, juked
the hallucinated defending team,
fouled out on stolen fixes.

His fiancée would check on him,
sing "The Tracks of my Tears"
and "Baby Love," want to know
where he was. A hooker stuck
in a dire life, 13, Candy found
her mainlining squeeze of OD.

The oblivious sun oozed viscid
blood through veins of youth.
I swept broken bottles, let
the sprinklers flow. Evenings
Jimmy soloed sax, the tenement
walls reverberated. In corridors
of acid, dim shadows caught
no break from the heat. Squad cars
shuffled streets fringing the fence,
looked lost, as if they didn't notice

the scores of teens hazarding
weapons, tossing their tomorrows
away for burgled merchandise
in the playground, as if they didn't
hear them rap revolution, see
gangs wielding sawed off chains
of swings, as if shots weren't fired,
and Bones never divvied dope.

## Puzzle

He gazes through a clouded window of silence
with no frame of reference,
softly pronounces a single word:
his name. This four-year-old, getting
younger in the eyes of his sisters who
are learning to read, and recite times tables,

is elsewhere, even face to face, doesn't seem to hear,
emerges when he wants something,
and if he doesn't get it, screams, kicks, bites,
then hides in a pandemonium of toys,
smashes dolls' heads like a mad drummer,
smears apple sauce, puzzles cookies
and cell phone to pieces,

withdraws to some remote region of darkness
where self can't grow.
We surmise frustration and chaos
overwhelm him when he struggles
to blend sounds. We have no remedy,
other than persistent work.

Mild and severe, the labels
have already started that will stick
like nursery rhymes.

We plan, improvise irresistible play
with counting and pantomime,
magnetic alphabet, puppets, animal books,
folk songs. I would lift him to learn the language
of the starry universe
if he would listen, show us how to help
multiply his everyday words

instead of stab at the paper, fling magic markers
and number cards everywhere.
He seems to forget, try less,
only wants outlines of his hand and foot.

I keep sifting broken, babbled words,
keep encouraging, bringing his senses to light.
We have to hurry. We want him here
to enchant us with all the ways he can give
and the sounds of the world he imagines.

## Fame

A kindergarten girl gives lessons in it,
knows that a hot pink bikini with shades
is the point at pool parties
where she wins gold in every race.

She *invented* leisure,
a dance and swim instructor
with a cake guaranteed to make the crowd
do her bidding.

When she strolls, servants fight to carry umbrellas,
bring lotion, lemonade, strawberry milk
to her *chaise longue.*

Paparazzi die for close-ups,
Oprah, Leno, and Riki,
leads on her next movie.

The chauffeur, a boyfriend,
speeds to Sunset Beach,
grovels to have the honor
of polishing her exquisite
toenails in time for ballet.

# The Boy Who Loved to Fish

He didn't fathom a word of English,
wanted his South Korean home.
*I don't know, I don't know*, he hid in fear

so his tutor gave him a map of Earth,
a recorder to breathe anywhere free,
become boss of whistles, Simon Says.

They explored crocodile rivers,
barracuda and marlin thrashed the seas,
trout sailed; the world grew less ominous

until another boy pushed him overboard
in school, and anger swallowed
the new words in his mouth. Life got sad.

With a calculator faster than the tutor,
he found laughter on an island
of numbers. Surprised he was back

the fish greeted him with singing,
chanted rhythms of English together,
introduced him to heroes from the planet

he needed to study, asked him to draw
muscular letters so they could play baseball
and golf, bike ride with feet on handlebars.

When the boy watered the tree he planted,
sentences sprouted like minnows in April,
he knew how to talk with every fish.

## From a Boy's Home

Spice gets nabbed with nude movies,
raps the FBI the real hotbed of porn
else it wouldn't be a snap to deal drugs
on the police precinct block.

He graffitis banks like roach nests
crawling with CIA crooks who juggle
books inside hidden vaults of the military weapons race
to embezzle billions for their pleasure
and launder money through loopholes to finance
the evil war on people of color.
We don't play a coin of their games,
wouldn't be stamped "disadvantaged" and "deprived"
if the government wasn't pimping undercover
crapshoots to promote commodity market fixes.

Gangs of buggy counselors clobber us
like an epidemic of clandestine terror
for protesting corporal punishment in our dorm,
and the schools tattoo our futures
"socially maladjusted" and "emotionally disturbed."
The sissy teachers say nothing. All they do is
dump crazy work in our faces
and drag us to chill with the dean
for quarrels a few hard cores fan into fights.

# Discovering Mortality

Death taps on the door, devil staff in hand.
A boy opens it, sees a skull of endless passageways,
counts the sardonic grin of presidential teeth.

I could get a galaxy of candy with a mask like that
the boy thinks. But Death bites a finger off,
says, "I will devour you." Blood running

down his body, the boy screams, "Please
kill my friend instead." "Perhaps, if you give me
all your candy at midnight," says Death.

So the boy drags a sack full of chocolate bars
pops and cookies, but Death lightning-snatches
the bag, then waves the staff into a scythe,
says, "Your head is dust, nobody lives forever."

The boy's mother watches. "Get inside
this instant," she orders, "the party is starting."
He walks in the house, blood leaks from the ceiling,
snakes over walls, he follows a trail of red footprints...

# The Hustle

Bet those dudes going home
scurry like scared pigeons
when I move out of the blackness
like a cat, hit on them
my car ran out of gas
three miles on the other side of town,
turf they'd never dare drive near.

I offer to mow their lawns,
do anything, for a spot of green,
and they fidget like they've got to piss,
look down the street
to see if their wheels are gone,
then up at the stars,
wishing I'd disappear.

Whiskers raps about a job
I could dig like a dog
all night in some gas station,
sounds more nervous than me
pretending I'm tired and sweaty
after escaping a gang of
rednecks out to beat my butt.

Beer Belly shuffles a marked deck,
deals me a joker to pawn my story
in the honky bar across the street,
as if I'm a bum, stupid enough
to get my meat handed to me
by 'hood honchos. I shake
my head no, dying to tell him

what to do with his smug tip
when, Poker Face, his buddy—
hasn't kicked-in a word yet—
busts the game wide open,
wants to check out the car key
if it's true I'm really stranded,
draws a cell from his pocket

like he's FBI, ready to call
the heat on me. Hell,
my motor's humming overtime
and I'm hungrier than a rat.
So I start to play like I locked it
in the car by mistake,
and then decide to stroll on.

# Advice from a Bag Lady

I don't pound doors, ring bells, or lie.
I wouldn't want *my* privacy trampled on.
So I knock softly, say *I don't mean
to bother you, but I'm homeless.*
With a friendly smile I ask
if they have a sweater or a scarf,
gloves or socks they don't wear.
You'd be surprised how understanding
people are. Sometimes they welcome me
into their homes, offer food and drink
since it's obvious I'm hungry,
even let me stay overnight.
No sense begging like I need drugs,
or lying that a car I can't afford
ran out of gas. I'd get as indignant
as they would if a hustler
tried to play me for a sucker.
And if they look disgusted like I smell,
or think I'm casing their homes
and slam the door in my face,
I turn with a pleasant goodbye
and walk on. No telling what interesting
folks live there. They might find
themselves in *my* shoes some day—
Who knows? We could become friends.

## Excuses

Sorry about my crazy spelling.
When I write the letters hip-hop
like a shell game and when I read
it's like some dealer pulling jokers
from the bottom—letters float
and jumble, twist and spin around
like when I ride the rollercoaster
and look weird in the wavy mirror.

Teacher says it isn't my fault,
the dyslexia I've got confuses
and disturbs me, gives me problems
adjusting. He never stops wasting my rep,
bosses us to read and write poems
in their flunky high school,

won't let us smuggle in soda
chips and candy, play the boombox
or cards during recess because Angel
tried to pawn a hot watch on him
then slashed his wheels for saying no.
I was ready to deck that punk, but today

Lucky got snagged carrying the knife
and Spice had to see the principal
for swiping an extra sandwich at lunch,
so our class blew the Friday pizza joint.

## Lunch Hour

Arm in arm they stroll the park:
the man, sixty minimum; the woman
twenty or so, pretty, and blind. She laughs
at something intimate I can't discern.

Her grandfather? friend? custodian?
What has he confided interests her that way?

I'd better mind my sandwich
and listen to this book,
not be a nosey squirrel sniffing the air
for a loose word as they walk by.
It's none of my concern if they dally
under a tree to whisper and conspire caresses
in the shade, lie down in the braille of grass.

Still, uncertain if the gray man
might be deceiving her,
I look over to the children on swings
and seesaws, splashing joyful banter,
would shield their eyes from the display.
But the children don't notice,

and when I go back to work,
memos and phone messages from the couple
are on my desk, the agendas of meetings.

# Siege

All night, freezing rain—the lights
won't make up their mind;
then everything's dark. Trees are walking dead.

In the tar pit of time, a transformer
groans like a dinosaur, becomes extinct.
The turncoat furnace sleeps.

Daybreak we are hostages of the ice storm,
light candles, stove, put a bucket
under the leak by the sliding doors,
resuscitate the fireplace, check for damage.

Storm—odd word for weather
so calm, where ice builds by degrees,
immures us inside a cold hurricane's eye.

The neighborhood is a breath
of blown glass. *Crack, crash*—trees discard
sodden branches. A dove is still
on a telephone wire of silver stalactites.

Debris is strewn over the battlefield
of tree bones. Broken limbs have toppled
the fence, could crush the roof.
We need a generator, radio batteries.
Is there enough food?

Wounded are throwing shivers
helter-skelter against the windows.
A transparent antler points
as a ghost staggers to shelter.

The phone's gone dead.
In a million offices, packs of wolves
circle, move closer, with fiery silver eyes.

# Empty

From Diamond Head haloed with contrails
to Honolulu, valorized hotels,
regimented as gravestones,
preempt the splaying fingers of surf.
Rest assured, however, the animals
are well preserved in their zoo.

We shuttle to malls
that slink the waterfront
with collateral condos
colonizing faster than coral,
view the USS Arizona, a hecatomb
for men uniformed in death.
Defeated as an island divested of wilderness,
the hull flags its life blood of oil
into azure reef,
angelfish haunt the breached turrets.

Sightseers decorated with plumeria
pay respect, browse souvenir newspapers
of the sacrifice. At eighteen-minute intervals,
a military filmloop salvages
a nutshell in the Memorial Theater,
takes the endless roll call
of soldiers who no longer obey.

IV

# Testamentary

*A man who dies without children...*
*It's as though he has ripped a page*
*from the Torah*—Rabbi in the film *Kadosh*

Father of the sacred blessing of a son,
these days of dwindling demise, our mother
in a nursing home with arrhythmia, dementia rending her
from memories my brother has honored,
        keeper of every leaf
shriveled to nothing and yet to breathe a fingerprint
of light, the grandchild she nannied since infancy
now a teenager, sings viola like David on the lyre,
        used to drop in from synagogue
and *shmooz* with her a widow twenty-seven years
unemployed, her Sheba wisdom bequeathed
the uncommon affluence of kindness, dividends
of their joy together, designated securities for tuition
        like Solomon, shared the chance
he might dream beyond diamonds and gold,
harness renewable energies in fluid pulses of fire
and the rivering wind's fingers of plenitude,
so the planet may heal, future generations prosper,
        yet my brother worries—
snapping a confiscated switchblade as we settle
down to dinner—her condition could linger,
he won't be able to budget the foster care facility
and college on probation officer salary,

       even if he orchestrated a secret signing,
amended securities and altered the trust,
it wouldn't change the *tzedaka* my sole sibling lived
every day next door to her, the treasure of being blessed
with his unswerving friendship, the indispensable handyman
repaired her car gratis, delivered groceries,
       managed estate affairs, drove her
often to the Cascades and Oregon coast she loved,
lightened the endless hours on inhalator and morphine
       till the ocean of peace.

Notes:

Kadosh: holy
Shmooz: talk heart to heart
Tzedaka: righteousness

# Renascent Elegy
*for Ray*

Astonishment. Your Manhattan address
immediate disbelief, winning a lottery
seventeen years after our friendship
separated, envelope windowed with stamps
commemorating life's phantasmal journey:
Missouri settlers meeting natives,
Marquette Explorer navigating pioneer canoe,
a stagecoach careering across the horizon
of Cherokee Strip, Antarctic Treaty,
Carolina Charter... We were travelers
on the treacherous train of new hope
going in various directions, finding
forgotten vestiges of selves. Long-absent

they bustled aboard, took seats beside us,
passengers with stories, carrying books,
briefcases that bulged dossiers and resumes.
An excited teacher told us he was
on the way to welcome a friend at the airport,
hadn't seen him since 1979; an attorney
stethoscoped a laptop for the news
as we bridged memories of fraternity days
at Baruch School, cherry blossom springs
in the Brooklyn Botanical Garden,

let dreams from deserted correspondence
cultivate a fragrant orchard in the future.

Reading "Asphodel, That Greeny Flower"
to you one night, after the lines...
"It is difficult/ to get the news from poems/
yet men die miserably every day/ for lack/
of what is found there."... it looked
as if you'd nodded off from the wine,
but the lowered lids were to listen better.

Dauntless judge, political maverick,
low-key connoisseur of ethnic cuisine
ordering Merlot and Szechuan,
handing squirrels sunflower seeds,
you turned me on to Borodin's *String Quartet in D*,
von Weber, Armatrading, alternative theater,
seduced the divorcée at Lake Oscawana
with tunes on guitar and showboat water skiing,

mailed the chance to plant in a field
left fallow, replenish dormant roots
connected to different experiences
eager for the fruition of companioning

wise gifts. Messages materialized instantly
every day and night at home stations,
we commuted poems with spirits of linnets
and bluebirds, calendared vacation time
to celebrate your imminent retirement
from courtrooms where you mediated fairness.

We were deep into the light of gleaming affinity
beyond the end of a subway tunnel when
fate's absolute gavel suddenly
derailed plans, reality's fury
jolted the fact of its opposed truth
down denial's larynx,
ashes in a fiberboard urn
inflamed emptiness,
and tragic forgiveness,
offered to the perjuring wind,
engendered sorrowful remembrance.

# Plans

An advocate against the tidal wave
that gulped Iraq, you left the apartment
five streets from Ground Zero
to winterize the Oscawana Lake house
where we loafed with poems
and girlfriends in the promiscuous 1970s.

You talked a good game: steady tennis,
songs on guitar, time with your son's baby,
volunteer at the veterinarian, freelance mediate.

You refused to don the judge's robe,
a gadfly in court with Woodstock dissent,
discovered abuse of power in the NYC
Department of Correction.
TV reporters followed the case.
*My five minutes of fame*, you said.

Knotted at the neurotic hip to a forbidding father,
his banker ambitions broken by Nazis,
you battled depressions with psychiatrists and drink,
couldn't climb out alive.

A trim 55, visiting a new woman,
you didn't think it would last.
*Say kind sentences to her*, you would counsel
when I got miffed about a failed affair.

You didn't have time to buy the piano,
begin the scathing book of scandals,
even our sets in tennis,
thought you could improve the snarled
unjust world with gentleness.

# Nest-Egg

Depositing inheritance from my mother
after her death, I see: Bluebird Houses $7
on a bank wall. Perhaps bluebirds will nest
in a house in her memory. Truth is she
didn't know a bluebird from a bluejay.
A doe nibbling the yard, a friendly cat
wandering outside alarmed her into a tizzy.

Resisting her large gifts was tantamount
to transgressing the fifth Commandment.
We knew never pull a wallet if she was present,
never talk back. Thirty grand she brought home
on a bonanza Vegas trip playing the slots.
Betting the trotters, jai-alai, card games,
any chance to kibitz, was her cup of coffee.

Very different from my wife who collects
coffee grounds for azaleas and rhododendrons,
shovels earth of veggie and herb gardens
with hands, bequests raspberry, strawberry
and blueberry crops, cultivates salvia
and Indian paintbrush hummingbirds kindle,
relishes risks wilder than icebergs calving.

Setting away disequilibrium and hypothyroidism,
my mother would spin us into dizzy irritation
and laughter. We relied on her to change
her mind. I see her smile now a woodpecker
taps the white oak and feathers of blue sky
perch on maple branches as if the vaults
of time unlocked and bluebirds prevailed.

# Doing Time

1943 to 1945 in Tonkawa internment camp
near Norman, Oklahoma, my father
served as an officer supervising POWs.
Unlike Nazi concentration camps,
facilities included a theater for musicals,
dayrooms for games and writing letters,
even a tailor shop, library, and orchestra.

Knowing Yiddish, a German dialect,
he buddied a prisoner, on the QT slipped him
cigarettes and Lifesavers, bent the bars
with pleasantries. The thankful detainee
asked him for wood, was handed
pine scraps sawed in the carpenter shop.

Hundreds of days deployed in a cell
like pawns lined up for slaughter
as the prisoner sculpted the kings and queens,
carved details of bishops and castles,
horses salient to break free, presented
the chess set I discovered in our basement,
sleuthing around when I was nine
and didn't understand my father's irascible
hatred of a country for the Holocaust,
the slavery of war.

"I would have killed Hitler," he said,
clenched fists holding back tears of rage,
the few times we squared off in a game.
To avoid the violent sorrow, I didn't salute
the subject of his alliance with the soldier.
And yet I wonder about their mutual interests.
Did he help other prisoners? Bargain
whiskey, beer, chocolate? Was the soldier
an officer? Did anyone find out?—
Pieces my father stowed away for good,
prejudice in checkmate, kindness redeemed.

## Fragments of War

David's stone, launched
with reluctance, deterred
Philistine armies.
Shot from the cosmic sling,
a meteoric rainbow
terrified foreigners.

The gunman aims,
a bullet screams
and faster than the gods
guided Achilles,
a body enters earth,
silent on impact
as the echo of an asteroid.

## Casualties

*I am the enemy you killed, my friend.*
*I knew you in this dark...*
—Wilfred Owen

The sea, relentless cavalcade,
devours soldiers on fleet incursions
of surf, wave after wave catapults
over reef, in phalanxes the tide
surges like battering rams, drills them
to the gates of cliffs; fuzz-faced recruits
who would rather note the swaying
targets of girls, and reconnoiter
news of gridiron rivalries, follow
uncivil orders to invade another Troy,

scramble over the wrong zone,
find victims never-ending, many
who don't want to be saved,
hurl stones, fire back tooth for
ballistic tooth; as the tide retreats,
the leviathan regiments
search the rubble for dead
mutilated and disappeared,
try to remember a cause,
see the enemy mirrored,
with charcoal eyes.

# That Mysterious Yearned-For Person

In the bedroom, blindfolded,
he half-regretted the agreement,
doubted this plan was worth
jeopardizing intimacy.

On the phone they were close
friends revealing taboo desires
and vulnerable secrets, imagining
liaisons of shared fantasies;
neither had thought to find out
the other's occupation, religion,
color of eyes, hair, skin.

The tentative, persistent footsteps
could have been anyone's
entering a livingroom she'd never seen,
where a nightlight soft as candleflame
showed contours of curtain,
a chair to lay her coat on.

They had agreed there would be
no words here. So noiselessly
she slid her shoes off,
turned slowly down the dark hushed hall,
glimpsed him in a far window,
back to her, unaware,
taking off his shirt—an illusion.
Only the build of his voice
was molded in memory.

Was it the nuance of her breathing
or his own heart-pounding arousal
he heard, motionless,
naked beneath the blanket?

The silhouette of a sleepwalker
moved through the doorway,
hands probing dark.
Then knees nudged against the mattress.
She stood next to him, beginning
and end of a fantasy,
unfastened blouse, bra,
skirt sighed to the floor.

He lifted the covers like negligee,
between them, warm waves of flesh,
scent of mocha and vanilla,
*do anything,* their unspoken whisper.

## Sunflower Fever

She planted a variety of registers:
tenors and baritones by windows,
altos and sopranos as you enter and leave.
Swinging in and out of radiant mouths,
bees rollick a razzmatazz of notes.

Combos she painted on canvas
blaze in the livingroom. Stems
like praying mantises and beanstalks
trellis to grassy cloudswirls,
lemon-orange rays flare auras
of banana fingers on fire, unwind

riffs of golden birds....

Designs on fruit bowl and thermometer,
candleholder, even the oven gloves
and coffee mug sizzle sultry motif.
*Summertime* solos of Coltrane and Pepper
soaring out of another world
with cadenzas steamy enough
to get eggs cooking like flying saucers
don't send her as far as the rays
in a seed of one sunflower.

She would dance their light forever,
down to the honeycomb
of an ear of corn.

## Vows

It bothered him getting mixed in with
errant exes who had betrayed her,
though she'd survived martial law Poland
married to an adulterer—the Solidarity leader,
imprisoned by *Milicja Obywatelska* during
her first pregnancy, left her the children
and zilch alimony in this unfamiliar society,
an immigrant with no English, employment,
relatives, or friends. Afterwards, she lived
with other cheaters, but they'd be nothing
more than wisps of his own past infidelities
if she'd believe in his brand of faithfulness
without the trappings, honor their love
exclusively, he would devote himself
to her language of pysanki, long leaf pine
needle basketry, breakfast with the rising birds.

And yet, middle aged, why not live together
*before* wedding? It was adolescent,
antiquated, coercive: ring or else goodbye,
she refused to give it a chance, tempted
with unrevealed promises of amazing
solicitude as a legal wife. He wondered
what she'd been holding back, scoffed at
the buttery bribes, imagined the step-children
with friends crashing his home, husband
caught in a web embroidered like a cathedral
quilt bedspread, caged as a stone pendant
in wired jewelry, a canned broadcast
about a childless, domesticated ex-bachelor
no longer free to wander and breed.

Like obedient children who haven't learned
to govern themselves, they registered
the insecurity of license and pre-nup,
composed ceremony and reception.
He had to live with his dream proven false
and practice a principle that has lasted;
she had to live with the fantasy of love
he would never divorce. Only too soon,
death cheated them into settling for less.

## On a Plane from Yellowstone

Maybe I didn't want to discover you as much
as anyone I have ever loved beyond snow-crested
mountains of cougar, forests of elk and moose,
river valleys of bison, bear, eagle.

We creep, a snail across a ceiling
of brilliant blue. Clouds like feathery geysers
convene fruitless questions:
Couldn't I love enough? Was I too selfish?

Had I met her a few years sooner,
the waterfall woman next to me
filling the vast void of your absence
with countless challenges,
you would have seen canyons
echoing rainbows in misty spray,

roots of pine trees dancing
in the grass with purple wildflowers,
the Mammoth Hot Spring Terraces
like gothic glaciers,
their limestone frozen cataracts
melded over sienna,

focused binoculars on a trumpeter swan
embraced by arms of sunrise
streaming hazy trees.

      Antlered with headsets,
homing in business agendas
and pastures of video,
our skein continues to watering places
of work, the refuge of parents.

Child I have never known,
all things are joined with light
flowing in words like blood.
I wanted to talk many times.

# The Claim

How quickly
the new snow
is claimed
by the boy who

before the sun
can melt a flake
or open his fathers
drowsy eyes

plants footsteps.